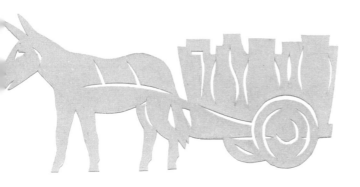

Diogenes the Dog-Man

Diogenes the Dog-Man

Narrated by
Yan Marchand

Illustrated by
Vincent Sorel

Translated by
Anna Street

Plato & Co.
diaphanes

Our story begins in Greece two thousand years ago, on Aegina, a small island in the Aegean Sea just across from Athens. Onesicritus, a rich citizen of the island, says to his youngest son Androsthenes:

"My son, you are strong, handsome, and no one can run faster than you or beat you at javelin throwing, but the most important aspect of your education remains lacking."
"What aspect is that, father?" asks Androsthenes, astonished to have more things to learn after so many years of schooling.
"Your soul! This is why I have decided to send you to Athens. Over there, you will see magnificent temples and the most beautiful sculptures in the world, but above all, you will listen to the greatest of all philosophers!"
"Of whom do you speak?"
"Of Plato of course! You will attend his school and become wise and learn lots of clever tricks to help you succeed in life."

The young Androsthenes grasps his father's hands and promises to work hard. But to be honest, he is simply happy to visit Athens, the marvelous capital of Greece. Some people call it a city of pleasure.

"But first," says Onesicritus, "go get your compass and your square and practice drawing right angles, for Plato refuses to teach anyone weak in geometry!"

Androsthenes makes a face because geometry is not his favorite subject, but he really wants to go to Athens! So he runs to the beach, kneels in the sand and traces all kinds of shapes: triangles, squares, circles... After several weeks of training, he is ready.

Athens! The weather is mild, and the city is dazzling and full of life. The inhabitants wear splendid clothes. In the Agora, the marketplace stalls sag under the weight of the merchandise. Magnificent temples tower in honor of the gods. On each street corner, there are very friendly inns where the best wines of Greece can be tasted. Androsthenes can already tell that he is going to like the city. But first, he must find Plato's school... While he is asking an Athenian for directions, something stops him: a beggar is walking about the marketplace brandishing a lit lantern. And yet the sun is already high in the sky! The poor fool cries out in the middle of the crowd:

"I'm looking for a human! I'm looking for a human! Although I have searched high and low, I cannot find one anywhere!"

Androsthenes raises his eyebrows and wonders who this strange person can be. As for the citizens of Athens, they lower their heads and pretend not to see him.

Plato's school is called the Academy. The building is surrounded by a vast garden. Plato greets the young man and begins by immediately asking:

"Are you at least a geometrician?"

Androsthenes recites what he learned by rote. He talks about angles, segments, areas and perimeters. Satisfied, the old philosopher authorizes him to attend his classes. The other students are already sitting on the benches, waiting. They look very serious. Then the teacher starts to teach…

"My dear disciples," Plato begins, "today I am going to talk to you about the ideal city…"

Everyone is taking notes. Androsthenes glances around the room; it hadn't even occurred to him to bring his writing materials. He understands nothing and can feel boredom creeping over him. And Plato talks on and on and on… for hours on end.

Androsthenes wants to cry out for help. He is hungry and hot. He is fed up with the ideal city and prefers to stroll around the city of Athens with its smells of the sea and of olive trees.

As he starts to nod off, he realizes that the beggar with
the lantern is listening to the lecture from a window. Plato,
who has also noticed the presence of the curious fellow,
throws him an angry look. The beggar starts laughing:

"What are you doing here, Diogenes? Stop laughing like that!"
Plato bursts out.
"Is it my fault if your lecture is so funny?"

The dirty, shaggy-haired beggar leans in through the window
with a mischievous look. Plato continues his lecture
unperturbedly. He opens the umpteenth topic of the morning
and starts to talk about humans, asking himself if it is possible
to define them.

"The human," Plato says, "is not a thing nor a plant. Therefore,
it is an animal."
"Yes, this is true," reply his disciples in unison.
"And can we say that this animal walks on four, three
or two legs?"
"On two legs," the students shout.
"The human is thus an animal that walks on two legs.
But be careful! Birds also walk on two legs but are not human."
"Oh no!" exclaim the students"
"So it must be said that the human is an animal without
feathers who walks on two legs."

The students applaud. Androsthenes is surprised to learn
that he is a featherless biped.

"Marvelous!" Diogenes cries out as he leaves with a snigger.
"O divine Plato, you enlighten me! Now I know I deserve to
be called human!"

Plato has been lecturing for at least half an hour when the beggar comes back with a rooster that he has carefully plucked. He approaches the philosopher and throws the animal on the ground:

"Here you go, O wise one, I present you with your human!"

The students couldn't keep from smiling. Humiliated and hopping mad, Plato starts to yell:

"You are so annoying, Diogenes! Leave us alone! And you," he snaps at his students, "stop sniggering like idiots!"

Plato cannot bear to be contradicted, especially in public. He starts calling everyone ignorant. Then he declares that classes are over for the day.

Androsthenes is delighted to leave the classroom. He almost gives the beggar a coin to thank him for his liberation!
He takes advantage of his afternoon off by continuing his visit of Athens. A sea breeze stirs the treetops. Women and men meander around the market. A crowd has gathered a bit further on. What a happy coincidence! Anaximenes is giving a speech! He has the reputation of being one of the wisest men in Greece.
Androsthenes doesn't want to miss this. But just as he makes it to the stage, Diogenes dodges past him.

The beggar has exchanged his lantern for a herring that he is waving around in the middle of the citizens. Alarmed at the idea of their nice clothes getting soiled, they rapidly disperse. Anaximenes, surprised by the crowd's sudden dispersal, falls silent. Then Diogenes exclaims:

"You see that, Anaximenes! You have the ability to create an assembly with your words. The herring has the ability to disperse it. Which of you is the greater? You, or the herring?"

Anaximenes turns pale with rage. A bald man, shocked by this provocation, cries out:

"Clothes smelling of fish are very difficult to wash! You, of course, don't care. Your coat is already so filthy…"
"I congratulate your hair for having left a head as ugly as yours," replies Diogenes before taking off to bother someone else further on.

Androsthenes, amused, asks the bald man if Diogenes is always like this.

"Always! We don't get a single day of respite. One can't do anything without him coming to ruin it all. But you haven't seen anything yet, my son! Once, in the middle of a crowd captivated by an orator's discourse, he lifted his coat and squatted down to empty his bowels. In this way, he showed what he thought of the speech…

Another time, he insulted my nephew who was receiving compliments on his beautiful wool coat, saying that it was actually the sheep that should be congratulated.

And one day, he pushed his provocations so far that some men started to hit him. In revenge, he wrote their names on a big sign that he hung around his neck. In this way all of Athens could scorn the cowardice of the noble citizens who ganged up to thrash a poor beggar.

Even in the stadium, he is unbearable. Instead of behaving himself and remaining seated, he rises to his feet in the stands to hurl insults at the athletes from every city! One day, he will go too far and will be condemned to death, just like Socrates!"

The colors of the setting sun caress the marble of the temples. The citizens chat in the coolness of the evening. Androsthenes walks along slowly thinking about the strange man, Diogenes. Suddenly, he sees the sign of a rustic inn. Didn't he come to Athens to have some fun? He enters and orders wine from the island of Chios, renowned as the strongest and the finest. As he brings the glass to his lips, a famous man enters the establishment: it is the great Demosthenes. His orations are marvelous, Androsthenes knows them all by heart. When he tells his comrades from Aegina that he has seen Demosthenes, no one will believe him!

Suddenly, the front door bangs violently. Diogenes has burst in! Demosthenes, afraid of being caught in a place so far beneath him, tries to hide in the back of the room. But Diogenes spots him:

"Look at you sneaking to the back of the inn!"

The band of drinkers bursts out laughing. The renowned figure, red with shame, starts stammering:

"I've... I've every right to enjoy myself!"
"Drinking wine with the scum of the citizenry, you call that enjoying yourself? Do these distractions make you happy, at least?"
"Definitely," asserts Demosthenes, regaining his dignified composure. "This wine is excellent and I am perfectly happy when I drink it. Come, have some with me."

"I could not afford such a small delight."
"Whatever do you mean? It will cost you nothing, be my guest."
"Tell me, how much suffering does such an indulgence bring with it?"
"None at all!"

"None at all! These grapes grew on vines, they were harvested, pressed and their juice stored in earthenware jars handcrafted by potters. These jars were transported on carts, which were themselves constructed by a craftsman. This wine crossed seas! It endured tempests and pirate attacks. And all these men—craftsmen, seamen—labored: their skin baked under a burning sun; they injured themselves with their tools; they broke their backs; some died by drowning or were sold as slaves—all of that for what? For a goblet of wine! So, tell me, whom does this wine please?"

"Um, well… me," Demosthenes stammers.

24

"You? But think how many days of labor this small pleasure has cost! And now that you have drunk this cup, I'm sure you are dreaming of drinking more expensive wine; wine from the island of Lesbos! And once you will have drunk the wine from Lesbos, what brew will you start desiring? The drink of the gods? The famous nectar of which one single drop brings eternal inebriation and youth? How many more days must you work to pay for this nectar? How many princes must you flatter to accumulate the money needed to purchase this beverage? How many friends must you betray to make a fortune? See how demanding your palate is! The least of your pleasures requires a huge amount of trouble."

"Diogenes, you have lost your mind! The pleasures of which you speak are really of no importance! I'm having a drink, that is all."

"A second ago you told me that this pleasure made you happy, and now you tell me that this pleasure is of no importance. I'm confused. Do you mean that being happy is of no importance?"

"You annoy me, Diogenes. What you say makes no sense!"

"I think that your wine is starting to leave a bitter taste in your mouth."

The customers of the inn are grinning from ear to ear. Demosthenes, defeated and ashamed, leaves the place without even touching his drink.

Diogenes looks around at everyone in the room:

"When I am thirsty, I have a drink of water. It is infinitely more pleasing than all your wines! What can be simpler or easier than to take a sip from a spring? I don't need to work or to make others work, to possess an immense fortune and to tremble at the idea of losing it. I don't have to mix with tyrants or anyone else. When I drink water, I know that I will be able to drink as much as I want for as long as I live. How ridiculous it is to desire wine, of which each drop is linked to a sea of tears!"

The crowd is struck dumb.

Diogenes comes up to Androsthenes:

"Hey there, I saw you at Plato's school! You must be intelligent
if you are taking classes from such a great master, so tell me this:
do you prefer to drink water in the cup of your hand or to have
wine come by way of the sea from the Island of Chios, to work,
scheme, compromise yourself and go to war, with the solitary
goal of tasting a drop of it on your tongue?"
"No doubt you are right," Androsthenes murmurs while lowering
his eyes. "The simplest is to drink water with one's hands."
"And being able to taste it as many times as I wish, without
asking anything of anyone, this is what is most pleasing! Am I
right? The other specialties, mixed with sweat, dangers and lies,
are in fact poisons."

"But no one can live so meagerly!" the young man dared to retort.
"Even the gods do not deny themselves a bit of comfort."
"But I do not want to imitate the gods! I want to imitate dogs.
This is what I want to become: a tireless beast, capable of
enduring all deprivations while rejoicing in the slightest of things.
My nectar is a bit of water when I'm thirsty. My ambrosia is a
crumb or a vegetable peel when I'm hungry! This is my delight!
And when I see men such as yourselves, wallowing in an inn to
gorge yourself with wine and thinking only of ridiculous pleasures,
it makes me want to bark and to bite you!"

The men do not dare reply.

"Dogs," resumed Diogenes, "desire only the necessities of life.
Water. Air. The warmth of the sun. The sweetness of fruit.
They want what is easily accessible and never lack for anything.
For them, the earth is a table of abundance and the entire world
their abode."

With these words, Diogenes leaves the inn. The drinkers, content to see him go, take deep breaths of relief. Androsthenes, fascinated by what he has just heard, no longer wants any wine. He thinks about the way of life described by the beggar: simple, pure, carefree. He murmurs to himself: "What if he's right?" He looks at his coat. What is the purpose of all that embroidery? He looks at his hands. What is the point of all those rings? Why be well-shaven, well-groomed and drink from a silver chalice? Does one live a happier life if one is well-dressed, stylish and perfumed? Is one happier if one possesses a nice house with furniture and slaves to serve at the table?

31

A bright moon illuminates the night sky. Androsthenes cuts across the roads of Athens. All is calm when a cry makes him jump:

"Calling all humans! Hey there, humans!"

Thinking someone needs help, the young man runs towards the cry. Who does he see? Diogenes, alone, in the middle of a marketplace.

"You again!" says the Dog waving his staff, "I asked for humans, not little runts!"

Androsthenes, offended, starts to curse, but the Dog, laughing even louder, says:

"You are no human, not a real one!"

The young man, cut to the quick, grumbles:

"And according to you, what must I do to deserve to be called a human?"

Without a word, Diogenes takes the young man's hands
and pulls off all his rings.

"Throw away anything that is not essential," he says.
"Keep only what you can replace easily and immediately.
At the beginning of my training, I owned some wooden
tableware. Yet I was still too rich. After seeing a child drink
water from the cup of his hands, I threw away my cup.
The next day, I crossed the path of another child who had
put his lentils in his bread. And I threw away my bowl!"

"Then you own nothing?" asks Androsthenes.

"Yes, me! I own myself. I have hardly anything but this coat...
I can't manage to do without it. It comes in handy in all seasons.
I can unfold it to wrap myself up in it when it is cold, or fold it
back up when the heat becomes unbearable. But I would like to
throw this away as well. One day, I am sure, I will live naked and
bear any climate. To achieve this, I train myself every day. In the
winter, I walk barefoot in the snow, and I embrace frozen statues
to acclimatize myself to the frost. In the summer, I roll naked
in the burning sand to learn how to bear the scorching heat.
That is all. I have nothing more to teach you."

"And the stick," Androsthenes asks, "what do you do with it?"

"It is not a stick, it is my scepter, for I am king."

"A king! Oh come on!" Androsthenes exclaims. "You look more like a beggar."

"Exactly. I am a beggar. I hate everything that other folks consider important: glory, riches, love. Yet no one can take anything from me, no one can give me anything, for I own it all. My only master is nature herself; she orders me to eat, to drink and to sleep. As for the rest, I obey nothing, I am my own boss. The Athenians have a fine word that indicates this state of sufficiency: autarchy. I am perfectly free. Who is freer than a king?"

Androsthenes looks at his rings on the ground. He asks himself if he shouldn't pick them up, go back to the inn and follow Plato's classes. But a question nags at him:

"You do have a place to live, don't you?"
"Right you are, indeed I do," replies Diogenes, puffing out
his chest, "I live in a palace. Would you like to see it?"

Androsthenes, curious to enter the Dog's den, accepts the
invitation. The two men walk across the sleeping Agora and
make their way westward until they reach the Metroon,
a high point of Athens where the city archives are stacked.

"Here we are!" Diogenes exclaims triumphantly.
"What?" Androsthenes asks in astonishment. "You live
in the Metroon?"
"What would I do with a marble floor, columns, cushions
and soft seats? No, my abode is here," Diogenes says pointing
at a large amphora.
"You live inside that!" cries the young man.
"You see how comfortable I am!" Diogenes responds as
he lies down in the container. "If you become a Dog, you will
have a residence every bit as beautiful as mine."

Androsthenes, with dangling arms, remains speechless.
Diogenes starts to yell:

"You hesitate to become a Dog! I see clearly that you prefer
your small comforts. Go back to Plato, that conceited man who
pretends to teach wisdom while wallowing in luxury, who plots
with tyrants to become a tyrant himself. Go back to him,
become like him, then tell me if you are happy."

The young man turns on his heel and runs away.

Once he arrives at the inn, he realizes that he has left his rings in the dust. "Am I any unhappier because my hands are bare?" he murmurs to himself. The next day, he abandons the school benches of the Academy. Many questions churn about in his head: should he pursue riches, honor and glory, as his father often told him he should? Come to think of it, his family members are rich and powerful, but are they happy? Has he ever seen his mother and father laugh together? No. Their brows are always furrowed with worry. No one ever knows which cloud has thrown a shadow over their minds. Has the time come to take the plunge?

The next time he crosses the path of a beggar, he takes off his coat and exchanges it for the poor man's coat. In a single day, he gives away all his money. Since he can no longer pay for the inn, he finds himself obligated to sleep outside. He shivers. He regrets his actions a bit. Then hunger begins to set in.

He wanders in the streets, bored and dying of hunger. He starts dreaming of a soft bed and a warm fire. Yet at the same time, he tells himself that he can do whatever he wants and go wherever he decides to go without having to explain himself to anyone. The Athenians look at him with a certain level of admiration, for one needs courage to live like a Dog! Androsthenes, leaning up against a column, starts to groan. He thinks he is going to faint but then Diogenes shows up. His face isn't harsh anymore.

"You just passed from childhood to adulthood," he says.

Then, to raise Androsthenes' spirits a bit, he tells him the story of how a mouse once saved his life.

It was in the evening, a long time ago, and he was eating
a lowly biscuit for his dinner. He sighed when he noticed
that a big party was underway in Athens. How happy all the
people looked! They were eating, drinking, reciting poems,
attending shows. He was on the verge of heading to the party
when he saw a mouse come over to him—it was feasting
on a crumb that had fallen to the ground. And so he
reprimanded himself: "Come on, Diogenes! Here is a mouse
rejoicing over a crumb, and you are complaining? If it can
be satisfied with so little, you can manage also!" The animal
reminded him that to stay free, one must first avoid
becoming the slave of one's stomach. For to have a party
and enjoy a good meal, it is necessary to work, to get up
when the master decides, to spend the day listening to orders
and only lying down when the master allows. And even the
master must obey other bosses in order to gain his fortune!
Androsthenes nevertheless asks Diogenes if this diet,
worthy of a mouse, risks destroying one's health.

"I believe," says the Dog, "that luxury, fat, flabbiness,
anxiety and bondage are much more serious diseases than
my scrawniness and my poverty. I think the real sickness is
to do whatever it takes to become rich."

However, something still worries Androsthenes:
fear of loneliness. He asks if the Dog still has friends.
Diogenes cries out:

"The Dog has the entire world for a friend! He has no king,
so he has no country. All peoples suit him! He never has
enemies. He likes Persians as much as he likes Lacedaemonians
or Thebans. He can go wherever he pleases, paying no heed
to borders. He keeps his arms wide open. His home is so vast
that he can welcome everyone. And this is true of all Dogs:
they call themselves citizens of the world, and not only of
Athens, Sparta or any random village. Are there any better
friends? I wish for nothing, I never fight to obtain riches, land,
or titles. I live, I meet people, I talk without worrying about
what others think. When I speak to someone, it isn't to obtain
special favors or money, to sell anything or to build my
reputation. I speak because I wish to speak, that is all. If the
conversation no longer pleases me, I leave. And I think that
people like my candor and my simplicity."

But Androsthenes has another problem. He has always liked women and he wonders what must be done to keep from falling into the torments of love.

"You desire love! But this is wonderful, my son! The only problem is that the couple is a complex invention that never fails to make lovers suffer. What efforts must be made to seduce, to understand one another; what negotiations are required to manage to live together! If nature had wanted us to live in pairs, she would have attached us at the hip. So here is what I advise: imitate the fish that rub themselves against rocks when they long for females..."
"But then," Androsthenes deplores, "the Dog cannot have children..."

"Wrong again!" declares Diogenes, "you will have thousands of them! The Dog gives the best education possible to each child, boy or girl, and not only to his own. I say that the ancient Lacedaemonians were absolutely right: they put all their offspring together, without ever revealing who was their father or mother and without ever telling the parent who was their son or daughter. In this way, everyone became the father or the mother of all the children and all the children became the son or daughter of them all. What a big, beautiful family! The Dog does not content himself with one, two, or three kids; he wants thousands, millions of them! As for yourself, I tell you that I love you like my own son, and every man of my age is my brother, every old man is my father, every old woman my mother. If it were up to me, I would celebrate the great wedding of all men with all women, and all the children would be communal children."

Emboldened by this advice, Androsthenes is decided—he wants
to live like a Dog. After training himself to bear the cold, the heat
and hunger, he begins to feel freer. Each thing, small though
it may be, starts to give him immense pleasure. What can taste
better than a drop of water when one is very thirsty, what more
satisfactory than a piece of fruit to a starving stomach? Several
months go by. The young man forgets his past life on Aegina.
But one day, while hanging about the marketplace, he finds
himself face to face with his older brother Philosykos. The latter
throws himself into his arms:

"Oh, my brother, you are alive! I was beside myself with worry!
You stopped sending us any news! I searched everywhere for you!
But how dreadful you look!"

Indeed, Androsthenes' fancy clothes have been traded for a beggar's cloak. His bare feet are black with grime. His hair, formerly curly and perfumed, has become a frightening mane that only a louse would want to touch. His sword, fashioned by the best blacksmith of Aegina, has been replaced with a staff crudely whittled from a branch.

"What in the world has happened to you? By Zeus! You have become a beggar!" exclaims Philosykos.
"Not at all," Androsthenes replies with a laugh.
"Then you have been sold as a slave?"
"Quite the contrary," Androsthenes says in a peaceful tone.
"I have become the freest man of Athens."

Philosykos takes a step back. He thinks his brother has gone mad.

Androsthenes refuses to go back to Aegina. He tells how
he became a Dog. His older brother listens carefully to him.

"Would you like me to introduce you to the one who liberated
me?" Androsthenes asks.

Philosykos accepts. They walk towards a large amphora. Curled
up in a ball like a dog in his kennel, Diogenes is inside sleeping.
Here is the great philosopher—thin, dirty and all huddled up.
And yet...

"How peaceful he looks," murmurs Philosykos.
"I would like to wake him up to have a talk with him!"

But Androsthenes warns him:

"Do not wake him up or he will hit you with his stick! His own
master greeted him in this way. I have often paid dearly myself
when I disturbed him for no good reason. He will make no
exception of you. If you want to keep your skull intact and
become wise, watch him live; he is a real-life show. Imitate him.
His philosophy is simplicity: all you need is to become yourself.
Stay at least until tonight and I will introduce you to him.
You will speak together."

A few days later, the older brother throws away his coat,
gives away his money and takes off his sandals.

In his turn, he becomes a Dog.

Plato dies. That evening a grand celebration is held in honor of the deceased. Diogenes, who was very attached to their bickering, is rather sad. He remains quiet. Androsthenes and Philosykos, on the other hand, take advantage of the occasion to reproach the Athenians for leading a life of debauchery. Suddenly, they hear:

"By Zeus, my sons, my sons! I have finally found you!"

The two brothers recognize their father, Onesicritus of Aegina. The old man is beside himself with joy; he leaps like a fawn despite his age.

"But what has happened to you?" he asks, looking at the appalling attire of his two boys.

"I heeded your advice," replies Androsthenes. "I sought after wisdom. I went to Plato's Academy to attend his classes. I even saw Demosthenes. But in the end, I decided to follow the teachings of a Dog."

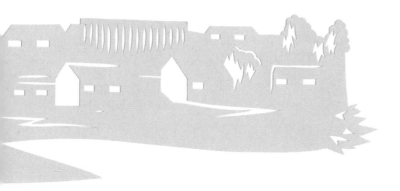

"By Zeus! A dog has become your mentor?" the father asks, taken aback.
"Not just any dog. The one I'm talking about has the body of a man."
"The body of a man! But what woman could have given birth to such a monster?"
"The woman's name is Philosophy and as for the monster, his name is Diogenes."
"Diogenes!" exclaims the father. "I haven't stopped hearing about him since I got here! Everyone says he is crazy!"

The two young Dogs look at each other and laugh.
How it amuses them to shock their father!

"That is quite enough! Now you are coming back with me to Aegina. I spent my whole fortune so that you could have the best education and look at the result! Beggars! That is what you have become!"

The old man grabs his sons by the wrists, as one does to little boys to drag them home. Androsthenes gives him a blow with his stick.

"Murder!" hollers Onesicritus. "My sons are killing me!"

Diogenes, who has been watching the dispute from afar, comes closer. He opens his arms:

"Come on now, listen to your dear old father! I have always wanted to go to Aegina! There must be folks to bite over there!"
"Excuse me? You actually think that I am going to bring you along?" asks the old man.
"If Diogenes comes with us, then we will follow you," say the sons.

Onesicritus is speechless with rage. But how can he refuse? He agrees to the deal and the Dogs climb aboard. The ship sets sail for the little island, but pirates attack as soon as it leaves the Athenian harbor. The crew is taken prisoner. Onesicritus cries, pleads and begs for mercy. They take his rings, his necklaces and rip his clothes. He shrieks as though they were ripping off his arms and legs.

"And the three of you", asks the pirate captain as he points to the Dogs, "what do you have to give?"
"Everything you need to make a real man out of you!" replies Diogenes.
"You won't find it so funny once you have been sold as a slave!" retorts the captain, surprised by such audacity.

They sail towards the island of Crete where there is a large
slave market. Onesicritus is devastated. No more riches,
fine food, wine or soft rugs! While he is lamenting his losses,
the Dogs chat together quietly as though nothing has
happened.

"But are you not afraid?" snivels the old man.
"Afraid of what?" asks Diogenes.
"Oh come on, you know, of being sold into slavery!"
"Oh, that!" sniggers Diogenes, "I'm not worried about that. I
am the servant of no one, not even of the gods.
I feel rather sorry for whoever buys a Dog of our caliber."

The pirates are exasperated. As soon as one of them shows up, the Dogs can't keep themselves from poking fun at him. And if they are threatened, they answer back that they don't care about dying. To punish them, their rations are cut, but they bear the deprivations with a laugh. They even share their food with the other prisoners. The crew can't understand how they manage to survive on so little. When the ship lands in Crete, the Dogs have a whale of a time: the moment they are off the ship, they start making fun of all the customers at the slave market. Diogenes shouts at the top of his head: "Who wants to buy a Dog?" Androsthenes says to a very fashionable young man: "Hey there, if you want a human in your house, here I am!" Philosykos hails a passerby: "For the price of a slave, buy yourself a master!"

Onesicritus can't help but admire his sons' audacity. He admits that no school could have given them so much self-assurance.

The pirates sell all their slaves except for the three Dogs and Onesicritus, who is too old. They don't know what to do with them when Diogenes calls out to a rich citizen of Corinth:

"Hey there, aristocrat! Buy me and I will manage your house!"

Intrigued by his insolence, Xeniades—for that is his name— decides to buy the little group. The pirates give him a good price for they are anxious to get rid of this pack of maniacs.

Onesicritus, impressed by the freedom that the life of a Dog offers, asks his sons and Diogenes a million questions. During the voyage that brings him to Corinth, he thinks over his life, of all the lost years, of his love for power and money. He finds himself ridiculous. Upon arrival in the harbor, he tosses his sandals into the sea. His sons throw their arms around him and kiss him.

Ten years go by. Onesicritus is a poor but free man in the company of his sons. Only he no longer says: "My sons." The sons no longer say: "My father."

As for Diogenes, he becomes Xeniades' friend and advisor. The sumptuous abode becomes very simple. The plush rugs and the richly embroidered clothing are all gone. The children learn to drink water rather than wine, to eat lettuce rather than beef, and to laugh rather than to plot and betray.

The story of Xeniades' house is told all over Greece. It even reaches the ears of a certain Alexander, the king of Macedonia and of all of Greece.

Diogenes, lying on the ground, is sun-bathing when
a voice calls out to him:

"I am Alexander. Beggar, ask anything you like from a king."
"You are blocking the sun!" snaps the Dog as he waves
his hand in the air as if to shoo away a fly.

And Alexander steps back. Those who witness this scene
can't believe it. Diogenes managed with a few words
what all of Greece had not managed to do with its entire army:
make Alexander retreat. The king, by nature quick-tempered,
retorts:

"How dare you! Are you not afraid of me?"
"Are you a bad king?" asks Diogenes.
"Of course not!" says Alexander, outraged.

"Then you are a virtuous king. And a virtuous king
is something good, right?"
"Exactly."
"So why would I be afraid of something good?"

Alexander is nonplussed but he admires the Dog's nerve.
He promises to send him a bowl full of bones as a reward.

"A gift worthy of yourself..." sighs Diogenes.

The king looks around. The Corinthians cannot keep
from laughing. The young Alexander admits defeat;
he stops puffing up his chest and leans down:

"I have killed men for lesser things, but by Athena,
you certainly have wit! If I were not Alexander,
I would want to be like you!"

While Alexander takes off to conquer Asia in search of
glory and riches, Diogenes remains in Corinth at his friend
Xeniades' home. But far from taking an easy retirement,
he pushes his training to the extreme: he decides to no longer
use fire in order to become a real dog, capable of devouring
his food raw. At first, he contents himself with crunching
vegetables, then with chewing grains. Wanting to toughen
himself even further, he starts to eat raw meat and encourages
the other Dogs to do the same. Everyone falls ill. Yet Diogenes
persists. One morning, observing what the fishermen have
brought in from the sea, he sees an octopus twisting around
in the bottom of a basket. He grabs it and takes a bite...

Diogenes is seized with violent stomach cramps and dies.
And this is how such a man, as strong as Hercules, Dog
among dogs, is killed by an octopus at eighty-six years of age.

Diogenes' companions ask themselves what should be done with his body. Androsthenes thinks they should throw it in the street for the dogs to feast upon. Philosykos thinks they should cook it up and share it among friends—indeed, Diogenes did say that human flesh is just as good as any other… it would be a shame to waste it. But Xeniades has the last word. Before dying, the Dog whispered his last wish. He asked to be buried… face down.

"What a strange idea!" exclaims Onesicritus. "Why face down?" "Because according to him," says Xeniades, "everything that is underneath will one day be on top."

No one knows if Xeniades dared to put Diogenes face down in the bottom of his grave, but in honor of this man who became an animal, in honor of this animal who became a god, in honor of this man who became a man, the citizens built a massive tomb superbly crowned with… a marble dog, always on the look-out.

French edition
Yan Marchand & Vincent Sorel
Diogène l'Homme Chien
Design: Yohanna Nguyen
© Les petits Platons, Paris 2012

With the kind support of

INSTITUT
FRANÇAIS

First edition
ISBN 978-3-03734-933-5
© diaphanes, Zurich-Berlin 2017

www.platoandco.net
www.diaphanes.com

Layout: 2edit, Zurich
Printed and bound in Germany